Some plants have found a way to solve this problem.

They have turned into meat-eaters.

Meat-Eating Plants

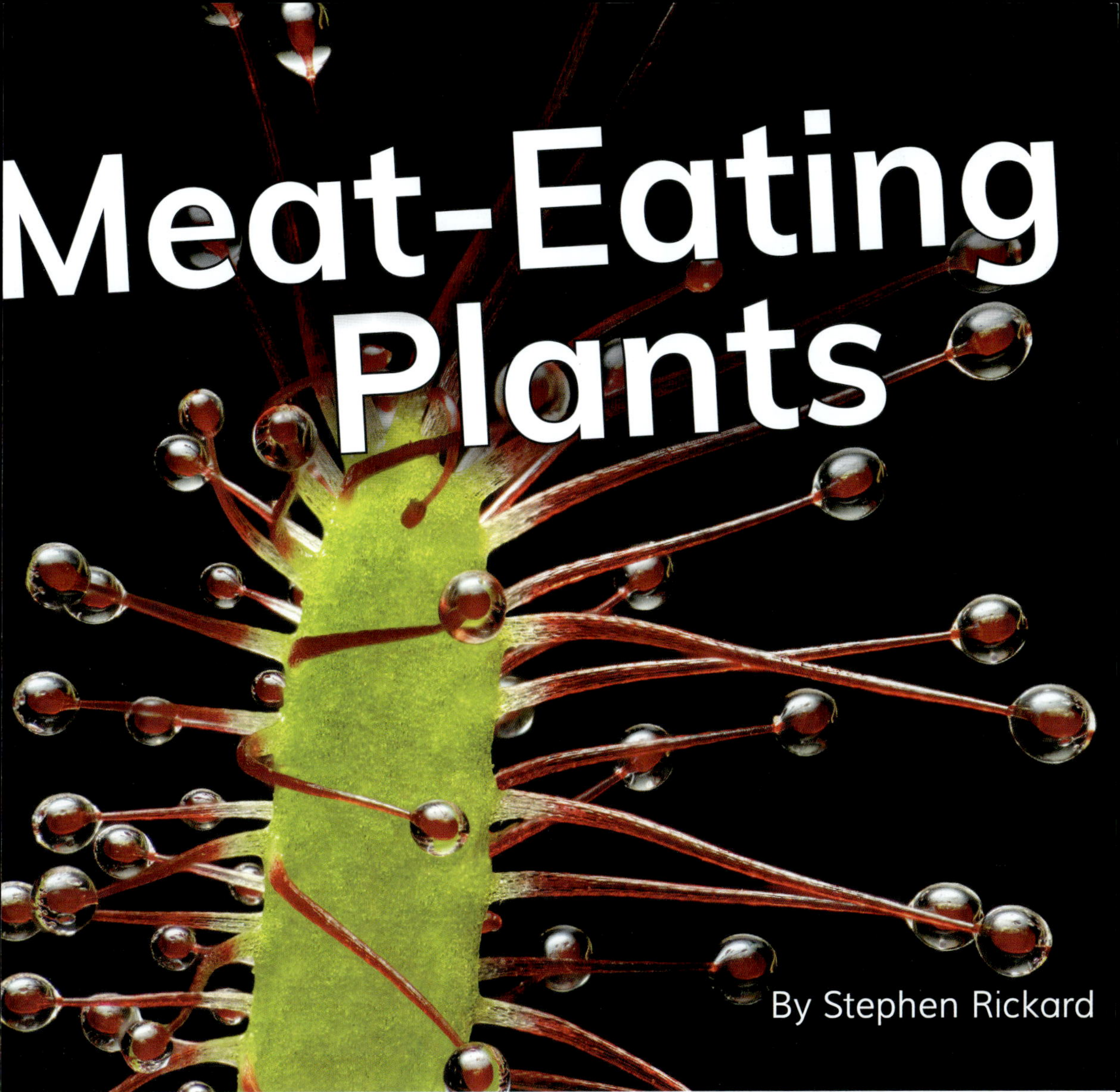

By Stephen Rickard

Published in 2026 by
Norwood House Press
2544 Clinton Street
Buffalo, NY 14224

Printed in the United States of America

Library of Congress Cataloging-in-Publication Data:
Names: Rickard, Stephen, 1957-, author. | Rix, Nicolas, illustrator.
Title: Meat eating plants / by Stephen Rickard. Tim to the rescue / written by Stephen Rickard, illustrated by Nicolas Rix.
Description: Buffalo, NY : Norwood House Press, 2026. | Series: Phonics all-stars: phase 5c
Identifiers: ISBN 9781978578449 (pbk.) | ISBN 9781978578456 (library bound) | ISBN 9781978578463 (ebook)
Subjects: LCSH: Reading–Phonetic method–Juvenile literature. | English language–Phonetics–Juvenile literature. | Carnivorous plants–Juvenile literature. | Superheroes–Juvenile fiction.
Classification: LCC LB1573.3 R534 2026 | DDC 372.465–dc23

CPSIA compliance information: Batch #CW26NHP: For further information contact Norwood House Press at 1-800-237-9932.

All plants make their food from sunlight and water.

However, to survive, plants need extra things as well, such as vitamins.

Most plants get these extra things from the soil in which they are growing.

What do the plants do if the soil is not good and it fails to give them what they need?

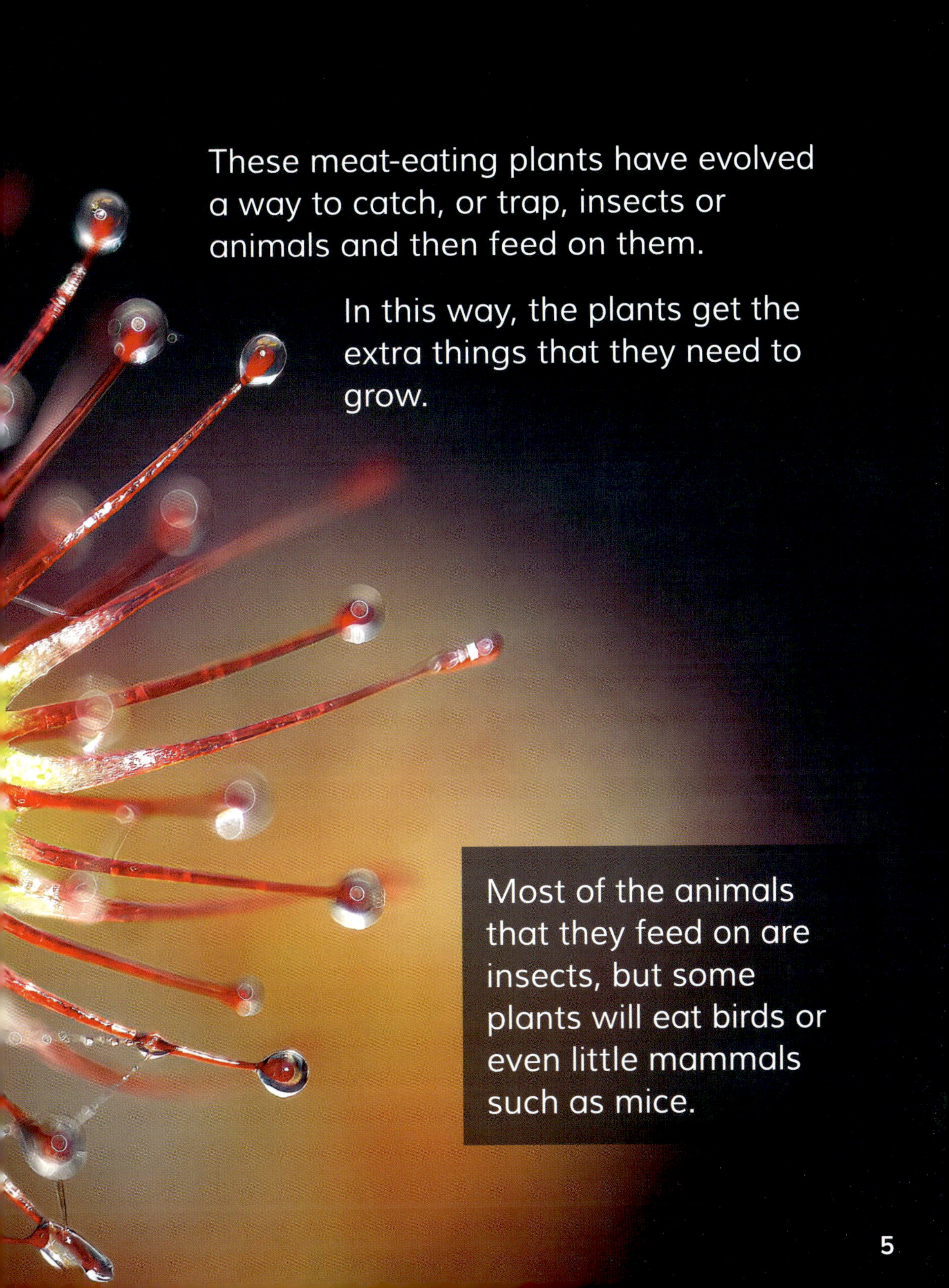

These meat-eating plants have evolved a way to catch, or trap, insects or animals and then feed on them.

In this way, the plants get the extra things that they need to grow.

Most of the animals that they feed on are insects, but some plants will eat birds or even little mammals such as mice.

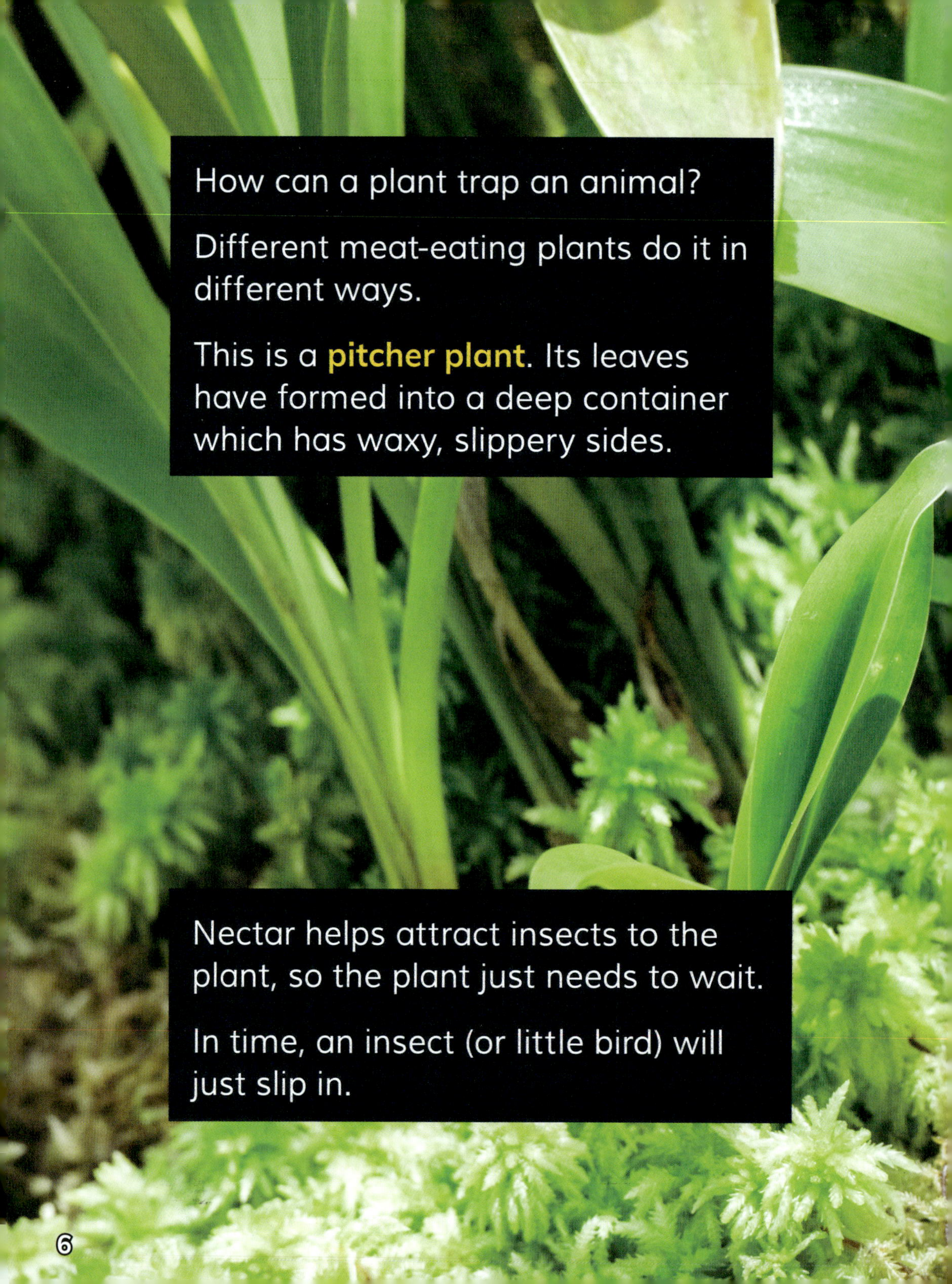

How can a plant trap an animal?

Different meat-eating plants do it in different ways.

This is a **pitcher plant**. Its leaves have formed into a deep container which has waxy, slippery sides.

Nectar helps attract insects to the plant, so the plant just needs to wait.

In time, an insect (or little bird) will just slip in.

Once the animal has plunged in, it cannot get out because the sides are so slippery.

The insect drops to the bottom of the pitcher, where liquid digests the helpless creature.

Some meat-eating plants have parts that are sticky, as if they have glue on them.

If an insect lands on the leaf, it gets stuck and cannot get away.

Then the plant can digest the insect.

This plant is a **sundew**. It is a master at catching insects in this way.

Some meat-eating plants have a kind of snap trap. This is a perfect design.

When an insect lands on the leaves, sensitive hairs on the plant "know" that the insect is there.

The insect acts as a trigger and the trap is sprung. The leaves wrap themselves around the creature so it cannot escape.

This sounds the death knell for the wretched insect. It is digested.

The **Venus fly trap** is the best known plant that can trap insects in this way.

Some people keep meat-eating plants in their homes.

You can do this, but the plants are very fussy. They need lots of sunlight and rainwater. Do not give them tap water as it will kill them.

Are any of these plants a danger to humans?

No.

At least, not unless they grow to a giant size and start to come after us!

Tim to the Rescue (Again)

Written by Stephen Rickard

Illustrated by Nicolas Rix

The bad dudes are up to their old tricks.
Come on, hurry up! There are loads of planets out there that need blowing up.
Bad dudes?

I said, come on – help me. Or we'll never destroy this planet.
You called us bad dudes. What do you mean?
Listen – we're not the bad dudes. That's not fair!

Look at that magnificent planet, glistening and resplendent in the sunlight.
Too bad it will soon be just a smoldering lump of rock.

Bad dudes ...

Meanwhile back on our home planet, Tim is on the job. There is no rest for the defender of the galaxy!
Yikes! I'm picking up an alarm signal. Good thing I downloaded that Attack Alert app on my watch.
That pair in space are up to no good again. It's time for me to stop them!

Go, Tim!
Whoosh!

Tim is meeting the bad dudes on their spaceship.
Now look, how about you both give me a bit of a rest? Saving lives all the time is getting so boring!

But we have to do this. Blowing stuff up is our job.
And you have to try to stop us. It's the rules.

Tim needs to get something off his chest.
Do you think saving the galaxy is fun? I really wanted to be a bricklayer. It must be very satisfying putting up homes and things.
But this is where I am.

But I just like blowing stuff up. Look!
Woo hoo!

I'll tell you what. We'll go to a different solar system and just blow up some planets with nobody on them. So you won't ever need to rescue anybody again.
How's that? Do we have a deal?
Bad dudes ...

Is that a good deal? Tim needs to see what people think.
OK, everyone. Deal?
Yes! Do it! It's a good deal!

So Tim reaches an agreement.
Right, no blowing people up – just deserted planets.
OK. Agreed.
Hang on ... we are the bad dudes!

Now Tim can live his dreams.
And he has a new assistant ...
Yay!
Pass the trowel, dude.